NATURAL WORLD

GRIZZLY BEAR

HABITATS • LIFE CYCLES • FOOD CHAINS • THREATS

Michael Leach

HODDER
Wayland

an imprint of Hodder
Children's Books

WWF

Produced in Association with WWF-UK

NATURAL WORLD

Chimpanzee • Crocodile • Dolphin • Elephant • Giant Panda
Great White Shark • Grizzly Bear • Hippopotamus
Killer Whale • Lion • Orangutan • Penguin • Polar Bear • Tiger

Produced for Hodder Wayland by
Roger Coote Publishing
Gissing's Farm, Fressingfield
Suffolk IP21 5SH, UK

WWF is a registered charity no. 201707
WWF-UK, Panda House, Weyside Park
Godalming, Surrey GU7 1XR

Cover: Face to face with a grizzly bear.
Title page: A curious grizzly stands high on its back legs to get a better view of the photographer.
Contents page: At full stretch a grizzly measures up to 2.7 metres high.
Index page: The humped back of this bear shows that it is a grizzly.

Text copyright © 2000 Hodder Wayland
Volume copyright © 2000 Hodder Wayland

Series editor: Polly Goodman
Designer: Victoria Webb

Published in paperback in 2001 by Hodder Wayland,
an imprint of Hodder Children's Books

A Catalogue record for this book is available from the British Library.

ISBN 0 7502 30509

Printed and bound by G. Canale & C. S.p.A. Turin, Italy

Hodder Children's Books
A division of Hodder Headline Ltd
338 Euston Road, London NW1 3BH

Picture acknowledgements
Biofotos 3 (Heather Angel), 15 (Heather Angel), 16 (Heather Angel); Bruce Coleman Collection 7 (Werner Layer), 9 (Leonard Lee Rue), 19 (Joe McDonald), 29 (Joe McDonald), 30 (Stephen J Krasemann), 31 (Johnny Johnson), 34 (Johnny Johnson), 38 (Joe McDonald), 39 (Erwin & Peggy Bauer), 44 top (Leonard Lee Rue), 45 middle (Erwin & Peggy Bauer); Michael Leach 13, 36, 41; Oxford Scientific Films 6 (Judd Cooney), 17 (Tom Ulrich), 18 (Frank Huber), 27 (Stouffer Productions /Animals Animals), 37 (Daniel J Cox), 43 (Daniel J Cox); Stock Market 14 (Kennan Ward), 22 (Ron Sanford), 24 (Tom Brakefield), 32 (Kennan Ward), 33 (Ron Sanford), 44 bottom (Kennan Ward); Tony Stone Images *front cover* (Stephen J Krasemann), 1 (Tim Davis), 10 Paul Souders), 11 (James Balog), 12–13 (Kathy Bushue), 20 (Daniel J Cox), 20–21 (Tom Ulrich), 22–3 (David Myers), 26 (John Warden), 28 (Barbara Filet), 35 (Darrell Gulin), 40 (Kim Heacox), 42 (James Balog), 44 middle (Paul Souders), 45 top (Tom Ulrich), 45 bottom (Kim Heacox), 48 (Daniel J Cox). Map on page 4 by Victoria Webb. All other artworks by Michael Posen.

Contents

Meet the Grizzly

A fully grown grizzly bear is one of the world's most powerful animals. Grizzlies may look slow and clumsy, but they can move quickly and can be very dangerous when angry. The grizzly is a type of brown bear. Its close relative, the European brown bear, can still be found in parts of Europe and Asia. Grizzly bears once lived all over North America, but today they exist only in Alaska, Canada and just a few remote parts of the American Rocky Mountains.

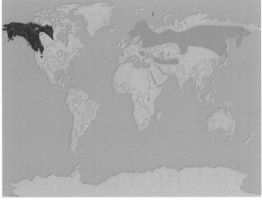

▲ The red shading on this map shows where grizzly bears live in North America. European brown bears are found in the areas shaded green.

GRIZZLY BEAR FACTS

A fully grown grizzly can grow up to 2.1 metres long and 1.3 metres high at the shoulder. Males (known as boars) can weigh up to 362 kilograms. Females (or sows) weigh up to 227 kilograms.

●

The grizzly got its name from its silver-tipped hairs, which can look as though they are covered in frost. In the past, 'grizzly' meant 'frosty'.

●

The grizzly's scientific name is *Ursus arctos horribilis*, which means 'terrible northern bear'.

▶ **An adult grizzly bear.**

Ears
Grizzlies have good hearing.

Nose
Grizzly bears have an excellent sense of smell and can locate food over a huge distance.

Eyes
Grizzlies have poor eyesight. They are short-sighted and have difficulty identifying objects more than 9 metres away.

Colour
Grizzly bears are usually brown, but they can be many other colours from cream and dark-yellow to black.

Teeth
Grizzlies have teeth that help them eat a big variety of food, including long canine teeth and flat molars.

Claws
Each foot has five sharp claws, which are used for digging, breaking open logs, tearing food apart and climbing.

Fur
Each hair on a grizzly bear has a very light tip, which makes it look as if it is covered in frost. This colour gave the bear its nickname of 'silvertip'.

Legs
A grizzly standing on its back legs is around 2.2 metres tall. When grizzlies stand up on their hind legs they are not usually being aggressive. It is more likely that they are curious and are simply trying to get a better view of their surroundings.

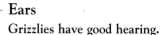

Grizzly relatives

There are seven species of bear alive today, plus the giant panda, which some scientists have classified as a close relative. Apart from the colour of their hair, all bears look very similar, but they occupy different habitats and have very different lifestyles. Grizzly bears usually live in hills and mountains. They prefer mixed habitats that contain woodland, meadow and fresh water. Grizzlies share most of their range with black bears. However the two species rarely meet because black bears are always careful to avoid their larger, more dangerous cousins.

WHAT'S THE DIFFERENCE?

Grizzly bears are much bigger than black bears and are twice as heavy.

•

Grizzlies have an obvious hump on their shoulders, whereas the black bear's back is flat and smooth.

•

A grizzly bear's ears are much shorter and rounder than a black bear's.

◀ Black bears are found over a far greater area of North America than grizzlies. They live in most of Canada and Alaska, northern USA and down the length of the Rocky Mountains almost to Mexico.

The only other bear in North America – the polar bear – lives in the extreme north. Polar bears spend most of their year wandering the sea-ice hunting for seals. In the short Arctic summer, when the sea-ice melts, the bears come on to dry land to eat grass, berries and shellfish. Polar bears never move from the coast.

The grizzly's other relatives live in tropical forests. They include the spectacled bear of South America, the Asian black bear of Central Asia, and the sun bear and sloth bear of Southeast Asia.

▲ The spectacled bear was named after the white marks on its face. Sometimes these marks surround both eyes to look like a pair of spectacles.

A Grizzly is Born

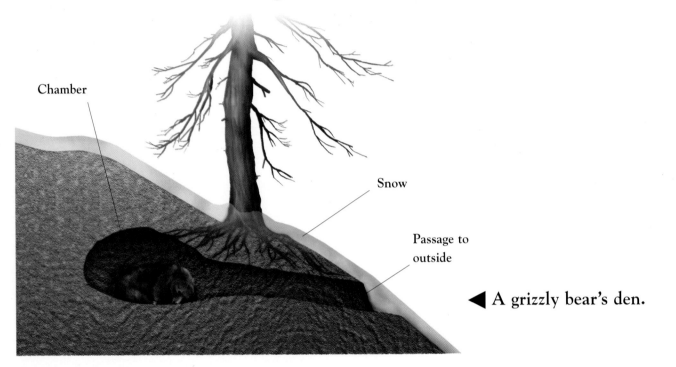

Chamber

Snow

Passage to outside

◄ A grizzly bear's den.

In the depths of a North American winter, a pregnant female grizzly moves uncomfortably inside her den. She is almost eight months' pregnant and about to give birth to cubs.

Grizzly bear cubs are born in a den underground, sometime between January and March. The average litter size is two, but up to four cubs may be born. The female sometimes has difficulty feeding and protecting all the cubs in a large litter. Only the strongest cubs survive longer than the first six months of their lives.

IN THE DEN

It is completely dark inside the den. The young cubs do not see their mother until they are about 15 weeks old, when they leave the den. Instead, they learn to recognize her by smell alone.

At birth the new-born cubs are bald, blind, deaf and completely helpless. When they are hungry, they give out a long, high-pitched squeal until their mother allows them to suckle. The cubs sometimes lie on a soft, warm bed of grass and moss collected by their pregnant mother in the previous autumn.

For the first few months of their lives, the young cubs spend about one hour a day suckling and the other 23 hours sleeping. They grow very quickly, fed constantly by their devoted mother.

▼ At ten days old, grizzly bear cubs still have their eyes tightly closed.

GRIZZLY BEAR CUBS

Grizzly bear cubs weigh less than 450 grams at birth and are about the size of a rat.

●

The cubs open their eyes at about 30 days old and can hear well after 14 days.

Leaving the den

When they are two months old the cubs can shuffle around. As they get bigger, life inside the den becomes more difficult. Soon there is very little room for the mother bear and her cubs.

The family must not leave the den too early. They need to wait until the big males have gone to the spring feeding grounds before they emerge. A male grizzly, hungry after five months' sleep without food would probably eat any young cubs he finds. So female bears always stay in their dens for longer than males.

The grizzly cubs first see the outside world at about three months old. By that time they have a thick coat of hair and well-developed hearing and eyesight. They weigh about 9 kilograms when they finally leave the den.

▼ Male grizzlies are a major predator of bear cubs.

◀ This Alaskan grizzly cub has only recently left the den for the first time.

The outside world

When the cubs first leave the den they are nervous and stay very close to their mother. But as they get older and more confident, they start to leave her side and explore further afield.

▼ Very young cubs grow tired very quickly. This one has scrambled up on its mother's back for a ride.

► Wolves hunt in packs. A grizzly cub away from its mother is an easy target for an animal that can run much faster than an adult bear.

Grizzly bear females are excellent mothers who will defend their cubs against any danger. But the cubs are never completely safe. A young bear that wanders away from its mother's protection might be killed and eaten by a passing wolf or mountain lion.

HUFFS AND GRUNTS

Female grizzly bears and their cubs communicate with calls. Cubs whine and squeal when they are hungry and produce short grunts when they are content. The female gives out a low 'huff' sound to call the cubs back to her.

▲ Female grizzlies spend a lot of time playing with their cubs. This keeps their relationship strong and encourages the young bears to practise their fighting skills.

Mother bears

Mothers with young cubs keep well away from adult male grizzlies, who will eat the cubs given the chance. Even the fresh scent of a male is enough to make a female turn and walk the other way. If they do meet accidentally, a mother grizzly will attack any male that threatens her cubs, even though he may be almost twice her size.

A mother grizzly with young can be one of the most dangerous of all bears. Anyone who accidentally comes between a female and her cubs is in danger of being attacked. This is why it is important to stay well away from bear cubs in the wild. Wherever cubs are found, the mother will always be somewhere nearby.

Female grizzlies are actually frightened of people. They realise that we are the grizzly's greatest enemy so, most of the time, females take great care to keep the cubs away from farms and villages. Even the sound of human voices can make her run.

▼ A young grizzly threatening a larger rival in Katmai National Park, Alaska.

Learning to Survive

One of the first things the young cubs learn once they leave the den is how to avoid enemies. Adult bears can run away quickly, but until they are fully grown, cubs have their own escape technique. When separated from their mother, cubs in danger climb the nearest tree with incredible speed.

Using sharp claws, the cub grasps the tree trunk and pushes itself upwards. In a few seconds it is high up where no large predator can follow. The cub stays in the tree until called down by its mother. Young grizzlies can climb well for the first year of their lives, but they soon become too heavy and clumsy. After the age of 18 months, they will probably never climb another tree again.

▶ Grizzly cubs prefer to climb young trees because they can reach round the thin trunk and hold on tight.

▼ Three cubs wait for their mother at the edge of a lake. Young bears are not always confident in deep water.